The Bare Plum of Winter Rain

The Bare Plum of Winter Rain

Patrick Lane

HARBOUR PUBLISHING

HARBOUR PUBLISHING
P.O. Box 219
Madeira Park, BC
V0N 2H0 Canada

THE CANADA COUNCIL | LE CONSEIL DES ARTS
FOR THE ARTS | DU CANADA
SINCE 1957 | DEPUIS 1957

Cover Painting, "Yellow Plums," by Phyllis Serota
Cover design by Martin Nichols
Typesetting by Smoking Lung

CANADIAN CATALOGUING IN PUBLICATION DATA

Lane, Patrick, 1939–
    The bare plum of winter rain

Poems.
ISBN 1-55017-226-3

I. Title.
PS8523.A53B37 2000   C811'.54   C00-910718-5
PR9199.3.L36B37 2000

Printed in Canada

In Memory of Dixie Lane 1914–1992

Her last words to me:
"At every turn there's always something lovely."

CONTENTS

WATER

Sometimes it hurts to be water.
Listen to the creak on clay, the lap
the water in the ditches makes, the way
it stirs in mud. I get down on my knees
beside water, listen to the drench and drone,
the thud a stone makes sinking in the clay.
And the water, because it sings
a song so old no one remembers it,
drags its beauty slowly. How hard
to carry so much inside.
How much it hurts to be water.

THE OLD ONES
(For Al Purdy)

He thought of the horses in January,
the old ones who had stopped moving
and stood away from the wind
in the leached coulee above Six Mile Creek,
snow and wind scouring their matted backs
and he wonders now what they dreamed
in the dead cold of that winter years ago.
Were they the horses who had loved
the steady pull of trace and strain, the long
journey in from Six Mile, buckboards
and wagons resting grey under the trees
in late summer, still hitched, standing
in the bare shade without water, waiting?
It was winter when he saw them last,
the old ones in the wind, their great heads
bent to spare grasses in the bleached coulee.
He had watched the wind crawl
through the horses' manes and tails
Even then he knew he'd seen the last
of their long journey to the town,
the blacksmith shop shut down,
the trees where they were tied
a lot for cars and trucks. The old ones
in their last winter, the ones who loved
the wagons and buckboards,
the steady sound of hooves in the dust,
the men and women and children behind them
talking their way to the stores and bars,
the hitching rails on Main Street, all that time
gone now. Still, they must have dreamed
or maybe it was only him,
balanced on his haunches in a frieze of wild rose
staring down at them and taking his body
among them for a moment,
snow cutting his eyes, the wind not yet
ready to die in those sagebrush hills
where the coulee lay below Six Mile
and the old ones waiting for it to end.

MORPHO BUTTERFLY
(for Mary)

They were not lost. The yellow butterflies who lay
their tongues on the drenched mud of a dirt road
found surcease in their flight. And that is old,
a story I'd have told when I was young.
It's not a deer upon the road, though I have seen
an animal fall into my lights and break
into fur or feathers, and then my stopping,
lifting from the broken grill its death. There is
no single memory. Every image flies
into my mind. So much of time is rest
after long wandering, and the wings that were
as much our bodies as our eyes, grow tired. Once
in my first manhood I stood in the heavy snow
that was a narrow cut of road and found in the broken
ice of a deserted shack a butterfly of blue,
so iridescent I became only mouth and thigh,
a warmth that might allow it life. There is a time
when the fragile falls into our hands and dies.
What high wind from Costa Rica blew such colour
into my hands and why was the breath I lifted
from my body not enough? A century ago
and still I dream of its small hands on me,
the mirrors of its wings. I saw myself
in the fractured glinting as it wavered on my palm.
Christ, it was winter. I was cold. You still
lay in bed with our first son in your arms,
your thin breasts bleeding milk.
I was building a highway in the mountains
so far away from my mind I don't remember it,
think now it was the way a body breaks itself
against what holds it, water falling into a vase
riding itself back to the stillness it was.
Nothing is lost unless we make it so.
I held that startled blue in the northern mountains.
I've held what I have held and every mark
the creatures made upon my flesh is totem
to what others would call scars. How terrible
when the flesh is torn, how beautiful the wings.

THE MACARONI SONG

I remember macaroni,
the end of the month,
the last week
when there was so little.

I made up
a song for the children.

The Macaroni Song!

Around the table
we would go,
laughing and singing.

Macaroni, Macaroni!

I can't make the song
work now on the page,
just remember, we
laughed so hard.

My wife stood
over the grey metal
where the macaroni boiled.

She never sang the song.

It was always six o'clock.

The children would cry:

Sing the Macaroni Song!

And I would sing.

One night
I stole three tomatoes
from Mister Sagetti's garden

and dropped them
into the curl of water.

My wife.
She loved me.
We worked so hard
to make a life.

Three tomatoes.
I still dream of them.
We were, what you
would call now, poor.

But when we danced
around the table,
my sons and my one
daughter in my hands
and sang the macaroni
song, God, in that moment,
we were happy.

And my wife at the grey stove
spooned the pale bare curls
onto each plate
and that one night
the thin threads
of three tomatoes.

I still dream of them.

Mister Sagetti, dead,
wherever you are
I want to say
this poem is for you.
I'm sorry I stole
your tomatoes.
I was poor and I
wanted, for my children,
a little more.

THE BARE PLUM OF WINTER RAIN

The instrument of your poverty
is an infinite departure, the hawk unseen
until you see him without prey
in the bare plum of winter rain.
He rests inside hunger
and he does not sing today.
How rare the gesture we make
with nothing. It is of the spirit and without
value. The bare plum, the winter rain
and the hawk seeing what you cannot say.
These steady accretions, yet allowing them
to stay as you stay with music after music
plays, and of course there is always,
always hunger, and, of course, poverty,
and the bare plum, empty, and the rain.

POVERTY

To put the little one, at last, down
and watch her fall into sleep,
the one whose face I touched
with bird fingers, bat wings,
the quiet strokes around the eyes
to still her.
My hands trembled from the hours,
the heavy labour. *I love you,
please just fall asleep.*
And my wife pretended to sleep,
her breathing slow, the kind that lies,
so the house, at last, at least, was quiet
and I could sit and stare into my hands
and wonder at how my fingers
put everything together, the thumb,
the fingers, the fingers, the thumb.

SAY

I got out of the car and walked into the fog.
She was dead. I felt what I felt
and there was nothing to say to them
except say, *Stay in the car.*
And then we drove another two hours.
The fog was still heavy in the low places
so that you wanted just to fly away.
What else to say?
I don't know if that is a question,
what it feels like to be a body
riding up over the hood
and rolling off the windshield.
So the cop said at the end,
What a night, and I agreed,
the kids asleep at last in the back seat,
their mother quiet. But, you know,
just to fly off the high places
when the fog isn't there,
just fly,
one of the kids, I think the oldest one,
saying, *Dad, did you kill her,*
Did you kill her? And just driving,
going on home, going on home.

OTHER DAYS

I remember washing her body as she said
over and over the one word, *No*, my hands
laving the cloth over her breasts and belly,
and the blood. I remember how blood,
when it is lifted from a body, becomes
another thing, and pale and pale
is as much thin water as a life. And
at each sound she made, that long *O*
turning around her still face, I said
Yes, as if I understood something
I didn't, the cuts coming clean like mouths
of children when you touch them with a hand,
their lips as bright as wounds, again
that word following hers, and now,
old, I don't remember whose word was last,
only remember her touching me
with the kind of touch the hurt ones use,
half-love and half-forgetting; *you,*
where are you now? And how long
must I hold you in my arms
as I carry you away again, your man
in the kitchen crying, the knife on the floor
waiting for whatever other life it had,
and our words ringing like soft bells
in the night when only the birds are asleep,
lost in the tired wings of that other day.

THE DAY OF THE DEAD HORSE

The day of the dead horse there was no rain.
It was hot on the iron cot, the bend of my body
stained on the stained sheets, the sweat still pooling.
The kids, the little brown ones, clambered over me
and told me of the horse who got killed by a truck.

They danced me from sleep. Half-strangled
by the sheets I fell onto the scuffed boards.
Mothers send their children to men like me,
strangers who sleep and do not work,
their own men gone into the fields to hurt themselves
with everything the fields give to those
who can't eat what they have grown. Such men
hate themselves with whiskey.
Cross-legged on the ground, the women
watched me as their children swarmed over
my body like small wasps with a need
only the mothers understood.

It was the day of the dead horse and someone,
a man, must cut it before it blows.
The heat turns the overworked heart
into a green wreck, the rot
already singing as the mottled eyes
caught darkness from the sun.
It was a lucky death in that village,
a strange horse wandered down from the hills
and killed by a truck. It was not a horse they knew.
I cut its throat with a knife a woman gave me,
the blade so sharp I thought the edge alive.

Cutting a dead throat is always crazy.
At least the living throat at its last heave
relieves the heart from wanting. A dead throat
is what the poor dream. With my cut the body
held its blood, the heart having blown
itself into the belly. The children
watched as the knife entered flesh.

Remember, I was dry drunk. It's the kind of drunk you have
that waits till you drink again, the kind that eats you,
the skin flowering with seeds that crawl like barley
under your skin. You don't want
a drink, you're only dry, a drink away
from what's been lost.
                          So I cut and cut again, stupid,
looking for blood and not finding it, cutting through
the throat and down into the chest, finding the lungs
and cutting deeper, splitting the chest
and lifting out the exploded heart, the smell of green
around me, flesh when it's gone bad.
How strange to look for blood when it's not there.
It was just a horse on the damned road
killed by a truck. It was a road that went nowhere,
not Damascus, not Ithaca, not anywhere.
South as far as Kamloops, north to Jasper or Prince George.

The kids watched and the women watched.
What lay in the ditch was food.

There are bodies so large only the earth
can hold them. I thought for a dry-drunk hour
I could feed them all with the heat-blown wreck.
I thought the death was mine to give.

I saved just ten pounds carved from the haunch
where the blood flowed least. The rest I left
for the dogs that are always there.
They seem to make us human. All the victims of our sleep.
I sat there by the ditch and thought I could make
out of meat a dream I'd understand.

That night I lay myself
in the dry salt-body of the iron cot,
so tired I couldn't touch myself or touch
another. The children watched their fathers
come in from the fields that were their lives,
and I knew as I lay in the stiff cushion of my sleep

they understood what I had done.
I lay there wishing I might have saved more,
that the knife could have healed the horse enough
to make of his body for all our lives a meal
that might have lasted longer than the one
we were to eat.

And the dogs howled
over the carcass, and the women seared
the bits the meat, and the men ate and fell into their bodies,
and the women wished a world where their men
didn't suffer so and the kids fell into a swoon,
their hunger gone, hiding
around the corner from the flies,
waiting until they too could sleep
in the healed and healing wounds that were to come.

COYOTES
   (For Eve)

My mother shot a coyote in the yard.
She wasn't used to guns and held
the rifle awkwardly, but she was tired,
her hens steadily dead she fed
her family with. He was grey
and I think now when he lay
in the dirt by the chicken yard,
tired. I would have just said
he was dead. He looked tired.
Burdens, misery, fleas and heat,
and loneliness I think now, an old man
coyote eating feathers as he died.

But I knew that coyote. Knew the bitch
who'd whelped his get for the five years
I'd watched their den. He would come
with that slow wallop of paws and drop
his hen at the broken mouth of the den.
He'd back off then and drop to his paws.
Fatherhood is wanting to eat
what's being given. Meat, you know,
the hunger in the hills.

She'd come then and he'd back off.
The pups would follow her, stumbly
and stupid as pups are
when they're barely born.
My father came home and cut the tail off,
then the ears. He was proud and angry.
It's like she didn't know what
she shouldn't do. It's like she shamed him,
like he couldn't look after what he owned.
Their bounty, one dollar
at the courthouse in the town: the stubbed
coyote my father dragged by one leg
to the dribbled creek behind the house
and dropped in the mud.

                    I remember back then
he was mostly tired. He said, when I stared,
Leave it alone!
                    As if I could.
I watched the coyote's body rot away.

I don't know what dreams are,
think when you hold a skull
you hold what most of us call memory
and isn't. I held his skull
after the body left. It was clean bone,
a pale, pale yellow, so thin
you'd think the maggots
left their colour as a mark.

I knew her den, knew
where she'd whelped his get. My mother
killed him in the fall. She hated guns.
The pups were grown.
I spent that winter crouched in my hide.
I watched her wandering.

She knew he wasn't there, but she still played
among the stones and dust where they had played.
When the new male came, all grey and wild,
she tore at him and then lay down beside
the wreck she knew his body would become.
That's what love is, I think, that lying down
beside what you know will die
and loving it no matter how you can.

They danced in the hills where she had danced
before. I watched them dance. It wasn't like
watching anything I knew. Her bite, her turning over,
her licking of him.
                    Under the moon
the tongue eats the heart away.
                              She went then
back to her den. It was the place where she had
whelped and licked a dozen into death.

His was a wanting he didn't understand.
He'd have eaten the pups as they poured from her
to fill her yet with what he had to eat.
He had the thin look coyotes have
when they know the lack of grouse and ptarmigan.
It's a look all edges, something crazed and gone.

She went to the den where she'd born his get
and ripped the earth apart. She sprayed the walls
and shat upon the ground and then, tail high,
danced back to him all toes and flanks and ears.

A mile away she dug her den. He watched her dig.
When he tried to help she bit him on the leg.
He waited then. He knew to stay.
It took her fourteen days. Five pups.

I remember hiding the gun. I remember hiding,
my mother in the darkness of the house.
In the dark must of that other den I've laid me down.
Dry shit, old piss, holes in the earth
a coyote makes to hide her blood.
How full a womb is when it wants
and how full the fierce when a coyote comes
to hunt among the hens for guns.

*Note: The words "his get" refers to a male's offspring.

DANCE OF THE WINGS

Every year my father nailed hawk wings
to the grey wall of the shed. He'd
sit me down by the chopping block.
My father worked in town.
The farm he'd been driven from
when he was just a boy was only memory,
something he hated, something he wanted to love
but he kept inside him what he used to know.
He pulled the small axe from the block,
placed his great thumb on the joint
and spread the wing. The dead hawk
flew in his hand when he brought the small axe down.

Once with a goshawk's wings
he danced in the yard by the well.
He held the wings and circled in a trance.
I thought he flew and flying
was the wind of those dry hills.
He nailed the wings to the shed wall
alongside the others who were dead.
The rotted ones had fallen away, nails
all you could see of wings
that once were there, hollow bones
like pipes of ice in the wrong season
littering the ground below the creeper.

I loved my father, knew he knew
things I would never know. The foothills,
Blackfoot and Kootenay, drift and far away
beyond the valley we lived in, prairie,
poverty, a boy thrown from his home.
I knew in my father's dance of the wings
he was back inside a century where birds
like hawks were things that had to die.
Rats, mice, cats and dogs, deer, moose and bear,
fox, lynx, the bobcat, anything he thought wild.

For him there was only the human.

There's a picture somewhere of us
standing by that wall. A man and boy.
It's years ago now. For me a century
that drags behind the century he knew.

But when you see your father dance with wings
when you are just a child, you know something.
Redtail, marsh, goshawk, peregrine,
all of these he flew beside. I fly too
but what I know I can't tell my sons.
It's my daughter who's learned
the death inside of life. Like women everywhere
she holds a skull inside her womb.

And the children of my children, well,
maybe if they came they could see me dance
in the garden, tranced,
no shotgun, axe, or nail,
no small one reeling on the wind.

THAT STRAWBERRY ROAN

What I want is the horses in the night, the storm
and me, drunk on potato vodka, my friend holding the bottle
to the light, his eyes full of the same squalid clarity,
the two of us stumbling into the wind
and the fire. The horses chased the pasture fence
like fists of love, that kind of yearning, that kind of want.
God, it was holy, and good and pure and right.
I sat with my friend among their thunder
as they raced over us without a touch,
the beat of hooves when they are wild.
It's like the earth knows what a window is
and rides straight through it. God,
when they came around the creek's bend
under the alders and ran through us, their hooves
a smell I carry in my skin, their sweat and fear
what I know of the night, young men,
drunk on their bodies, no woman near us,
bare to the waists, our chests and shoulders
shining in the startled cold of rain. We wanted nothing
but the bottle and our hearts. Horses
who sprang into fire from the sky,
vodka sweet as flight, like the neck we wring
in fury, an animal asleep in our wretched hands.
What else but love and horses
riding over our young skin. There is
the need to have such pain rain down on us.

THE NIGHT OF MY CONCEPTION

The night of my conception I wasn't there.
My father searched among the broken boards
and the dust of the rooms, my mother
behind him, her hand on his heavy back,
her mouth urgent, whispering, *Find him,
find him.* My brothers cried in their cages
behind the wall. I can see my father's hands
now, the swollen fingers as they picked among
small sticks, the fragments left behind
in the shack below the Sullivan Mine,
the silver lying deep and the zinc and lead,
the snow falling and the trees leaning to him
beyond the window as if they could help
in his search. *Find him, find him,* my mother
cried, and my father, crying now, lifted grey stones,
dug down into the earth that was their home.
My mother's hair settled on him like sound
settles on the floor of caves. I wanted to help
but there was no time. I lay between
my brothers, my small hands touching
their mouths, the open holes that were their song.
Soon, I said, *soon,* and when they had fallen
into the thin light of their arms
I went to my father and gave myself
into his hands, into the dark
of my mother's only body, long and white.

FAMILY

My oldest brother is a wasp
cleaning his body on a bullrush
above the pond's still water.
He is almost ready to take flight.

My sister is a thin white stick
in the clay pot by the kitchen fire.
She is so still only the dark can hear her.

My youngest brother is the first leaf
on a wisteria vine in spring. Already
he is thinking of winter, the colour
he will become before he falls.

My father is the woodbox in winter.
All the split and broken pieces
wait there to burn. I must never open
the heavy lid, must never look inside.

My mother is a wren looking for a nesting-box.
In her beak is a cotton thread, a blade of grass.
But there are no trees in this sparse land.
Where is there a place for her to rest?

I am none of these things.

I am the empty chair
at the bottom of the garden.
It sits deep in the shade
of the ponderosa pines.

There is no one there.

I GO IN WITH DEATH

I

I go in with death, knowing nothing
but the heart, the little one that beats,
the one gophers carry in cartilage and bone.
I am meat and I wait for the eating,
some animal like me, gnawing my bones.

It is what keeps me tense, the way
it wants more. Some other thing
come to bother me. Hell, a chickadee.
She gives me hell, wearing her feathers
to my slipping on wet stones.
Strange how lonely isn't, bewildered
by love and by regret.
                              And here,
and I can't stop this now, the hawk's wings
on the shed wall. A boy nailing flight to weathered wood.
My father nodded with the kind of *yes*
that came from the practise of years.
The angle of his mouth was the harmony
of goshawk and redtail, the way
their feathers became my hands.
The cry still torments and hurts the hand.

II

A hummingbird wing is what I hid.
I found the clot of colour hanging dead
under the wrong clouds. My father knew
there was something wrong. I
held its sharp wings under my tongue
as I nailed for my father the hawk's wings down.

III

My father was much alone.

IV

I nail him here.
I nail his hand and arm
to the planks of my eyes.
They are warning to what
wanders near, someone
who flies, someone
who dies, arms bent,
fingers splayed.

V

Go now, try to give me something more than
the harrier riding his wings through goldenrod,
the gopher running inside its blood. Or my father's
wrist rising with the axe and dropping
steel on the thimble joints of the shoulder,
the wing coming away, still flying.

V

And what am I to make of wings?
Almost to die, beaks and jaws, the men lying down,
their women in the kitchens at the stove
shaking their heads at one more thing dead.
It's the way spilled blood crawls toward flies.
Late in the afternoon a child could stumble
out of the sun with a dead gopher in his hands,
trophy to what he thought he would become.
Stones and withered grass. *Come to me,*
the dead cry, everyone asleep, some man,
old in the night, thinking with regret
of the whisper a snake makes
when you tear its skin off to make
a boot or belt, laughter in gone rooms,
fear, so long ago, the kill of killing,
the shoes I walk in someone's skin,
the pores remembering a single fly,
skin twitching, what my mouth remembers,

two wings resting on my tongue,
the shed wall, grey, south facing,
finding with a boy's small hands
the cartilage at the joints
that took the nails.

WHITE WATER

I want to write my way out of town.
I want to write all the way to the river
where my brother and I sat on a cold hard day
when we were driving Cat on the new highway.
I want to eat the lunch we ate that day,
baloney sandwiches - bread, margarine, and baloney
and cold coffee we'd saved from morning.
I want to leave a crust for the grey jay
who landed on my hard hat.
I want to sit alone on the high cold rocks
and watch my brother where he lay
in the tired loneliness of his bones.
I want to write my way there so I can say
to the rough and tumble of water
two boys who were men sat here,
and while one slept the other watched
a deer come out of the trees
to drink at the white water.
I want to write my way out of town
just for one day. I want to feel the sun
my brother felt, asleep. I want to know
what it was I knew as I gazed
at the delicate mouth of the deer.
To drink at the white water.
I want to write my way.
I want to drink at the white water.

APPLES IN THE RAIN

I return from the rain, bearing in my hands
the fallen apples, rusted and tired from their lives
among the branches of the trees I remember
and do not speak of but in song. They are
the ones whose limbs have sung
and singing gave their fruit to me
that I be made whole. Death is never a surprise.
I am surprised by life, and the holes my friends
made in me when they went away are the ways
small creatures find their ways back in –
moles and mice, and the cry of the midnight heron.
I believe even in the dark. The gift
I have been given is to see what's left behind,
a hand upon a woman's face, a mouth I touched,
a footprint on a stone. What else but song?
What else to draw me through the rain
only to find a child, apples in his hands,
finding what he can of his own way home.

THE LAST DAY OF MY MOTHER

I ask myself what I did on the last day of my mother
and now no longer know, think only of sitting with her
in the mall next to the Home in that last month
and lighting her cigarette, her hands still strong
though they trembled in the way hands do
when they go through an act of remembered delight,
obsession, addiction, her eyes bright as the jewels
my father couldn't give her.

I had pushed the wheelchair into the smoking section,
her urine bag swinging below her, the smell of her
dirty diaper, and when I told her we should go back
to change it, she told me to go on, people moving away
from us, ashamed, embarrassed, then both of us
smoking. The cheap coffee, the smell of her bowels
emptying the tables until we were alone together
as we had always been in our silence.

Tonight I don't know how to take these lines and make them
poetry, anymore than I could change my mother
who still looked upon me as a child, someone
she delivered in the night in the far mountains before the war.
I tried at the end to talk of the past and she admonished me.
*Why do you keep going back to those times? They're dead
and gone. Your father, your brother, all the dead .*
And then, *When we go back we'll play "Spite and Malice."*

But I don't want to turn this into metaphor, that childish card game
I played and lost, the sharp and vicious look she'd get
when she played me to a standstill
and then her glee when I paid her card for card
in nickels, her scraping the coins into the jam jar she kept
by the television where *Jeopardy* blared,
and when I didn't know an answer to some question,
said: *You're not very smart for a poet.*

In the bed beyond her an old woman lay in a coma,
the ward cat sleeping on her chest. Dead in her living body,

she had lain there two years. *That cat won't come to me,*
my mother said, her lipstick pulled across her cheeks and chin,
the last few hairs pulled down in a bang over her forehead.
I counted them one day when she slept and then, ashamed,
cried into my hands. That last day I changed her
diaper, took a cloth and cleansed her thighs and sex,

and thought of the place I'd come from, those legs
spread, her pain, the opening where my eyes first found
what light there is, her quick silence, my first cry.
Now she has grown tired of me, grown tired of us all.
The Black Widow. I called her that for years until
it was a joke between us, her telling me to stop,
both of us finally laughing, thinking of the desert
we had known and the spiders in the basement's heavy dark.

These lines have become a stumbling web as I move now
slowly toward my death. But I don't want to turn this
into a lament. Death is in us, it's how we're born.
She was impossible, implacable,
strong as a desert pine. Old lines, old poems,
her singing them when I was just a child:
"...By the Nine Gods he swore
That the great house of Tarquin
Should suffer wrong no more..."

Now, that's poetry, she'd say, and I can't make it, not like that,
not like the hours of childhood when she sat upon my bed
and put me to sleep with the thousand lines she'd memorized
when she was a girl. I was a child then, as she was still
a child, not safe in her father's arms in a memory I know
nothing of except as story. *You're so gloomy,* she told me
once. *Did nothing happen that wasn't dark?* And then:
What's wrong with you? What's wrong?

Sitting as she slept inside her flesh, reading Dickens
aloud, *The Old Curiosity Shop,* her favourite, the sounds
of that other time, that century slipping through
the smells of the ward, the carping woman in the bed
beside her, the other woman who slept forever with the cat,

and another who rocked her hours alone, no visitors I ever saw,
Dickens taking us all down the lost streets of another time, and
knowing she heard even as she slept, her mouth gaping.

I carry her in my flesh, can smell her if I try. No,
not the diaper, though that's there too, along with powder
and lipstick, and the trace of something I don't understand,
a smell from birth, or maybe from her breasts when I suckled
there. Something, nothing, a remembered thing from when
there were no words and everything was touch and smell.
Perhaps it was her womb I remember, that small salt sea
I grew in like a fish. And there, I've made this into poetry.

What else can I do? She carried me in the clutch
of her blue bones. My father put his ear to her belly
and said he heard me singing. She placed her hands
under that curve and held me before holding.
There's more than just the dark, she'd say, and it was
as if she'd said, *There is no death,* as I write and break
these lines again and again, letting them fall where they lie.

OWL

A saw-whet owl in the garden this morning
coming upon my mother's death in the far city.
We send whatever we can with all the hope
that we be understood. *At every turn*
there's always something lovely. My mother's last words
and that night-bird staring out of the dawn,
her small claws clenched around a mouse upon the lawn
and I wondered what she thought. What does an owl see
when she finds you in her eyes? Perhaps a man
in first light wandering among the things
he knows and does not own, a chrysanthemum stone,
the Emperor bamboo, a goldfish hanging in the shadows
below the shadow of a koi, still in the last cold.
The owl had come out of the darkness to rest
among bronze needles and scattered, bitter cones.
Fly away, little one.
I will listen for your wings in the night to come.

IN THE SMALL BOX, ASHES AND AN OPAL RING
SHE WANTED WITH HER, MY MOTHER, IN HER DEATH

Death is like walking through deep water,
something that resists and gives way
so that to raise your foot, to bend the knee,
to place it forward on the giving sand
is a great effort, the foot placing itself
and the body moving forward, the water
on your chest and belly a wall
that shapes itself, immovable,
as it moves sluggish as quicksilver
in a curve beside and behind you
in whorls that twist themselves
into quiet again, and the foot rises
again, the knee bending, and the arms,
held out of the water, descend
and move forward in fists, and the body
leans into that thick walking, only
the head above it all and the face,
the mouth open, breathing heavily,
the nostrils wide, and the eyes staring
at wherever it is you are trying to go.

THE WARD CAT

The man in the hospital who, late
in the night, the women, sick, asleep
took off his clothes, folding them neatly
and laying them down, the shirt and pants,
the socks and underwear, and the shoes
side by side beside the white chrome chair,
in a room with only a small light
burning above each bed, lifted
the covers and lay down
beside his wife who had not wakened
for two years from the coma, and
placing his arm across her breasts,
his leg upon her leg, closed his eyes,
silent, still, the breathing of his wife,
his arm rising and falling with her life
while the ward cat who would sleep
only with her, watched from
the foot of the bed, one ear forward
and the other
turned to the sounds of the distant city.

THE MADBOY

Every day the madboy runs
up the street from the Home,
his heavy feet hard on the pavement,
his arms flailing, his blonde hair
wild in the sun. He has slipped
from some door or window,
some crack in the wall only he knows
and now is free to run. As he goes
he keeps looking back at his pursuers
who follow him into the sun.
In the boy's face is both glee and terror.
He knows they will catch him.
They always do.
If there is fear it is the thought
they won't come after him
and will go on making breakfast,
flipping pancakes and bacon
for the other boys locked
in the bodies of men who crowd
the morning table at the Home
and he will finally make it to the corner
and be free. It is the place he never gets to.
The boy slows as his pursuers come on.
They walk slowly in the morning,
quiet, tired, knowing this is just
the beginning of another day,
and the boy will wait for them just short of where
the road breaks. And now he is happy
as they hold him in their hands.
He laughs at the run he's made again,
his face lifted up into the sun reflects
the knowledge he knows is his,
that for him the only escape is surrender,
that giving himself up is his whole life
and the room they will take him to
is a place where he can hold himself
sure of the great journey he has made,
bound once again by a locked door and the glass

in a window where he can see himself
among the thousand cells of wire embedded there,
knowing in his single mind there is nowhere to go
but into the arms of those who want to hold us.

BARENQUILLA

A dog, bright with hunger, forages in the light.
There is too much wonder in me.

Tell me, if you can remember nothing else,
At least my name.

ROME

There's not enough room in the small world of the heart,
and when the words came he felt almost happy, even
though he knew they were old words from another century,
and that their rising out of him was the way memory is a trick,
words coming out of the cornices and cul de sacs of his mind.
There were no bars this side the Tiber. Christ,
you'd think they would have thought of thirsty pilgrims.
He had tried climbing the many steps to St. Peter's
but there was no faith in him and his body, drunk
and shaking, would not go. So, he decided to pray there
on the stones of the square where millions
had prayed before him. He did not trust himself.
An old woman dressed in black stared at him
and he began to be afraid. She stood in the dismay
of someone's death so he pretended to pray harder, balanced
there on his thin knees, his hands raised up to his face.
But he thought his hands weren't quite right
and he kept adjusting them, moving the fingers
carefully so they would look exactly
like a man who had come to pray at this precise spot,
a spot where, perhaps, his mother had died, or a woman
he had loved for many years who had succumbed at last
to the riot in her bones and flesh. He
remembered then a Jew he'd known who swayed
when he was chanting. He began to sway,
thinking if she thought he was a Jew
she would somehow forgive him though
why he didn't know, and he chanted in what he thought
was an unknown tongue, something he had made up,
a child's tongue full of vowels and fear and he looked out
from the bruise of his right eye, the one
that sweated blood, at the old woman dressed in black
carrying, he thought but wasn't sure, a broom or spear.
She stood in what seemed to him now early morning
though he knew it was evening and day almost gone,
and she was old and beautiful in the way old women become
when they no longer want men, and a song crept out of him
ludicrous and old from The Salvation Army Sunday School

he'd gone to as a boy. It was an old song from his childhood
that started with the words: *Climb, climb, up Sunshine Mountain,*
but he couldn't remember the next lines so he just kept repeating
the one line as if it were a prayer or incantation
and for a moment he thought he was on such a mountain,
a mountain made of sunshine he might have climbed
when he was a boy and there were mountains, and the brightness
around his hands was more than he could stand,
his eyes hurting, and when he opened them
into what was left of light, the old woman was gone
and he was alone in the great square.
That was when he thought of the words that had begun
all of this, the words that came before he was on his knees,
and wished he had pen and paper to write them down,
but he didn't so he committed them to memory,
thinking he would write them when he got back
to wherever it was he had come from,
but he couldn't remember where that might be,
somewhere on the other side of the Tiber,
so he said the words carefully to himself
as if by repeating them he would be spared
the ignominy of where he was, knowing
he had pissed his pants and was ashamed and old.
The warmth on his thighs turned cold
against the gabardine. The words he spoke
somehow made sense to him, and he felt
he was in his glory and felt this was the moment
his life had been prepared for, and then there were hoses
sweeping the great square clean and a very old horse
grey and staggering on stiff arthritic legs
near the steps, and he wanted to stay there
until the waters washed over him and wished
the old woman dressed in black were still there
that perhaps she might then
come over to him and bless or curse him,
the saints nodding above the great square
and the horse lying down now. He knew
he could talk to the horse if he could get to where
it lay in the long shadows but the water sluiced in gouts
across the stones and the day was gone

and the old woman and the horse and the thought
was gone and he was alone with his shaking hands
trying to remember the line that wasn't there.

THE CHEST
In memoriam: Gwen MacEwen

The lock is heavy, embossed with gold
in a filagree as intricate as the weave of metal
in a Japanese sword-guard from the Ninth Century.
It hangs from its hasp as silent as a wasp in winter
that waits for the warmth of a hand to wake it.
Dragons and phoenixes guard the corners of the lid.
Their dance is carved, their dance is woven wood.
They stare at a dark sun who never moves
from the centre of the lid. It is a closed eye
in a country I can never travel to. Inside
are all the masks I have made of my life,
each one perfectly preserved, each one
waiting to come alive again,
to lift to my face so I can dance.
The steps are intricate, learned
when I was a child and my legs
were light as snow, as quick as ice.
I practised the story of the dance
until it became the eaten sun, the dragon
we call sunset, the phoenix we call dawn.
The chest waits for me.
Find the key, open the lock, lift out the story,
the one that ends with a gilded mask,
begins with a Japanese sword hilt,
a single image that moves me to the hidden,
the reminder of a sword, the hand's guard,
the one who writes me into the violence
of *My Lord, You.*

THE FLOOR
(For Peg Crozier)

On my hands and knees I know you.
Before they walk on you, before they know
who you are in the slip and slide of wine and laughter,
before all this you spoke to me
at the end of the day, your oak, your pine,
your slate, your tiles. You told me
the story of my knees and hands, you
said yes to the wash and wax and wane of me.
You shone in my last hour. You said
I am the beginning and the end.
I am what is made to stand upon.
I am the shining. And how I left you,
aching, full of the pain of my day,
my hands and knees, polishing and shining,
the temple beautiful, the cries of the pilgrims
as they fell upon what I had made beautiful, the one
who gave them with her body a place to stand.

THE BATHROOM

To be cleansed, to take your body in your hands,
to bend and shape its flesh, its teeth and nails,
to wipe clean the cock and ass of you,
the eye and ear and mouth of you, to touch
the lips and eyes and know there is no touch
like yours, the single pores, the scars, the hidden
solitudes, palm of hand, sole of foot,
the arcs and crescents of lines
that mark fate, love, and life,
the mount of Mars, of Venus, Jupiter,
and that faint light, Uranus, who sings his song
in the constellations of your hands,
the stars and moons in this hiding room, the one
you lock when you're a boy and your mother
wants to come and wash your hair
and for the first time you say, *No*, and she knows.
Then you are gone and she begins to hide,
beneath the carapace of motherhood some grief
you never understand. This room
where you sit and read the poets,
the smell of piss and shit rising around you
in the privacy where none may enter,
the single hair on your wrist you stare at,
so strange and beautiful, and how you touch it
with your fingertip and feel your flesh move.
Alone, exquisite, you stand,
and you cover yourself with the dead
skins of animals and plants, comb your blonde hair,
stare for a last moment at what has now become
a stranger, the one you will give to the world.

THE TABLE

Here we are at the end of day sitting around the fire, keeping as warm as we can, our shoulders almost touching we are so close. It is winter and cold and the animal the men brought home is finally burned. Everyone is tired – the men from their long day hunting in the snow, the animals they missed, arrows broken, an ankle twisted, one of the young men dead, his body far from the fire, lying broken from his fall in the snow – and the women, their bodies tired from the day of children and breasts and milk, and the digging down through snow for crystal berries made of ice and winter. No one thinks of a table. They squat on the earth. Now is the time of food, the time to fill the mouth with frozen berries and charred meat. It is late. The night comes and a girl lies down under skins, her body full of light because she is too young for memory. She curves her back into the cup of her mother's hip, bellies against the hard muscles of her father's arms. The child dreams. Perhaps it is a table, perhaps a bed filled with the down of birds, perhaps a window with yellow curtains and the image of an animal sleeping there, a lion or bear, a queen or king of beasts. How far away we are now! Think of an impossible table, think how we sit in this child's imagining as we eat our roast beef among candles and napkins, knives and forks, a glass of wine, someone's hand reaching for cranberries, someone's knee touching another knee under the idea we will someday call a table.

BONE CHINA

I thought when I was young
fragile was a woman's bones and flesh,
her life so delicate to touch it was to break.
I imagined it like a teacup.
You know, an old one,
bone china, the kind our mothers
wouldn't let us hold.

BEAUTY

Once you knew you were beautiful
but you don't know that anymore
which makes you even more beautiful.
The most beautiful women are the ones
who don't know. They are why
men lie down beside them in the strict observance
of grace, wanting to be a part of such forgetting.

THE BODIES ONLY BODIES

My children lay in the crouch of my belly,
their bodies only bodies, born, I thought,
before they should be born, all head and shoulders,
eyes all salt and dreaming,
so that the first time I touched their mothers
after birth I had to imagine this place of the sea
and, gentle, gentle, the mothers gave themselves to me.
I wake sometimes with memory,
and think a child has struggled into bed
as my small daughter did, who braced
her shoulders on my back and pushed
her mother out of bed. Or my sons'
fat arms and legs that would grow lean
and hard as a man must be when first
he rises into the smell of a woman's thighs.
But it is in the crouch and tremble of my belly
I remember them, my huge body rolling in bed,
and their sleeping over, under and around me,
safe as a child can be
when what is dreaming them
remembers in its story a father's flesh.
And the child when placed
back in bed, rolls into sleep
and the father finds in his arms their mother,
her quiet hands, the shudder of her arms
as she pulls him into her, again,
to that place he came from, crying
into the world the child he was.

YOU FALL INTO LIGHT

Someone loves you in the brief glance
the moon is when she rises. Look at the light
as it holds the needles of the solitary pine,
the single feather above the sudden eye
that is an owl at rest, her prey
hanging from a fist of claws. Your face
is salt and water. An argument for dream
is as brief as the glance the moon gives.
It is the single touch you reach for.
Behind you your lover sleeps
and you are standing on the back steps.
Every moment is as brief as this. The owl
rises on soft wings. The moon falls.

THE BRIGHT HOURS

Whatever changes, changes back to you,
the hours and days, the nights when I'm alone
inside the dark and time is what I knew
when stumbling down the miles of fallen stone

in search of anything but me. Long years ago,
and I still wander there though the tiny wren
who stares at me in the half-glow
of the opening day did not know me then

and wonders only why I stare across
the air at his bright eye. And maybe that
is what I once called loss
thinking myself alone and cold and flat

as any man could be. Now every day
is all I'll ever have, and night
a darkness in the heart so that I pray
for the only sun and the bright

forgiveness of a single bird now gone.
I know the wren dreams morning too.
Where do we go and for how long
and what in our making do we do

when words are all we find?
Yet the wren returns as if he knows
the question on my mind
and sings of stars and crows

to heal this hour I cry.
There is no place to go that is not time
and nothing I can do but touch your eyes
and know that what you see is the hand's climb

through loneliness, this braille of love
where what I touch is the body's sign

and nothing in the night that I can leave
now that your bones lie breaking inside mine.

THE SPIDERS ARE BACK

The spiders are back. How I love them,
these dream-catchers who weave in the night
the nets of morning. I have spent the last days
watching them draw out of themselves
a long story, the circles becoming smaller
and smaller until they rest in the centre
of the day. What makes us turn to such imagining?
The ones I see in spring
among the maidenhair and maple are so small
I don't know they rest on me until
I find them on my hands, sure that where I go
is where their web will be. Then they drop off,
the mothers of the fall to come. But what
do the males do, those stuttering dancers,
their legs so long? Do they have webs?
Or are they solitary wanderers, waiting for their time,
thin hunters in the green worlds.

Anyway, a question in the garden today. Love,
their webs are everywhere.
                              Fierce dreamers!

I think of them in my loneliness, and I am lonely,
have been all my life, but though for what or whom
I do not know. Perhaps the spiders know,
their bodies as much emptiness as air.

But, little bones, I broke today in the arc
of such silence I thought the world was made
of web and wandering, walked like a man walks
when he is alone.

Yet such days are pleasure when I bend beneath
webs and waiting. I take off my glasses,
bring my eyes to the spider

and we stare at each other in the day.
I would show you if you were here.

Blind, I've seen such things!
                              If what we know
is what resembles us, what we know is a garden,
the moment when a spider worries the dead
into a carapace of web, then rests upon
what will become her only self, the eggs
everywhere inside her. Somewhere
her mate hides in the green shadows.
As he waits he plucks a single filament of her web.
He hopes she will still long enough
for him to place his seed in her, then drop
as she turns to consume him.

He falls like a pebble from her jaws, his death
as close as that. Yet what music he made
she made for him. How I loved
him plucking the walking strings, her waiting,
as I wait here, to go, to come back to you.

HOW SMALL LOVE IS
  (For Lorna)

You're small, no, say it, short, a woman
who turns the day around, who turns
and turns upon imagined bones. Your flesh
is flesh, as much a cleft bereft as the turning
a rose makes when it unfurls the first
pale leaf we call a petal. I am undone
by the small mound you are under a simple sheet.
I touch your feet with my mouth
so you will remember me when you run.
You're round and round again, so many
curves my mind's undone by wandering.
I hold your bones in my hands.

Does the word *little* offend you?
I stroked a wasp once into stillness.
You understood. It's why my hands tremble
in the darkness of your hair, the gentle
place the inside of your thigh is, high up,
as much a filly's tenderness, so strong
it could break a man. The curve of your belly
you think old. How you let me cup it now.
Your last eggs glisten like forgotten grains
in the sand outside a silo. I've known each one
in the menses of your last blood, tell a story
to the child we never had. It always begins
with *Once Upon A Time.*
                    There is no once,
there is no time. You are small, admit it,
but like those holes they say there are in space,
you are a stranger kind of star. You are
what I see in the eyes of deer in spring.
Everything I know, reflected.
They shine in light. Dark stars, far spring,
the weight of smallness, how it takes

what I forget and turns who I am
to the opening of rain on old trees.

CUNT

I take from your cunt a cherry blossom at dawn.
I take from your cunt a cat in a cradle.
I take from your cunt sweet basil, rosemary, thyme.
I take from your cunt willow and pine.
I take from your cunt the crow's wing, the raven's song.
I take from your cunt the wolf's paw, a pig's hoof.
I take from your cunt the moon's laugh on a nail.
I take from your cunt the violin-bone of the fly.
I take from your cunt the hummingbird's tongue.
I take from your cunt the beetle in amber.
I take from your cunt a doll without eyes.
I take from your cunt river-stones, sea-glass.
I take from your cunt the blue stone's thin heart.
I take from your cunt an unborn walrus tusk.
I take from your cunt the little sequoia nut.
I take from your cunt the lost finger-bone of a mouse.

And you say, Don't stop!
You have forgotten the corn, the blackbirds in the corn,
the apple's star, the owl's feather, the little slipper.

There is more, you say. There is more.

VULVA

Vulva, you are the song of the little boat.
You are the moon remembering.

Vulva, you are the flutter of many soft petals.
You are the wavering, the unfolding.

Vulva, you are the clam and the leaping minnow.
You are the water of the blue stone.

Vulva, you are the whispering of the solitary dove.
You are the moth's wings opening.

Vulva, you are the open mouth of praise.
You are the cave in the silk mountain.

Vulva, you are salt water, you are the clenching.
You are deep water, the fish in the only well.

Vulva, you are the coming, you are the return.
You are the willow leaves in the wind.

Vulva, vulva.

THE DEAD OF WINTER

In the morning light the willow trembles
and mirrors sing. Last night my woman
imagined what a man might be
if he gave up everything. I believe
in simple stories. When we least imagine
there is music. Fragile cups of sound.
Imagine song when a tree is bound in ice.
You know that ice, willow ice in spring,
straw ice. The kind you take apart that sings.

CHICKADEE

Late night and the moon doesn't answer me.
What if all the stories were there just
to make us fall asleep? What if the night
was a man dreaming himself asleep, and the weave
was a mother's wanting, a half-dream, the kind
that keeps a woman awake in the sullen arch
she calls love and calls down upon herself
the last stars and says to herself:
This is the moon in my belly,
and rocks herself awake with her hand between her thighs?
What if this is the moon, her ass flaring white
in the night I reach for and enter,
and the whole darkness is only wanting?

There was a man who, when I asked him of love
said he wanted every woman he saw
and I said to him, *But that is only desire.*
What of love? And he looked at me long,
standing on the deck among the drift,
the men and women moving through their lives.
Desire is only style, I said, *but what of form?*

And turned away
and went to the moon which is *rabbit* here,
and *man* in other tales, and sometimes, *in extremis,*
just the moon. One night a chickadee fell into my lap
and I climbed the tree and put her back
on her perch, she who would admonish me
the next day in the morning delight
of black sunflower seeds, and who, if I asked her of love
would say, in the pursed lips of chickadees, that sweet
slide of lip on lip, the breath inward, calling,
would say, *There are no stories but that*
which held me in the night, fierce fluff of only air,
she who stores everything under the sun
and when the moon calls, calls it the waste of time.

THE GARDEN TEMPLE

Tell me every detail of your day—
When do you wake and sleep, what eat and drink?
How spend the interval from dawn to dusk?
What do you work at, read, what do you think?

P.K.Page, "The Answer"

No one comes to this garden. The dawn
moves through the bamboo beside the bridge.
It's quiet here and I'm alone. The small nun
who led me has drifted behind the screen
and I'm quiet as I watch a slender mallard
drift on the pond into first light. She is two birds,
one above and one below. Night and day,
and night was long again. You are far away.
Tell me every detail of your day.

Now more than ever I miss your hands,
your small feet, the slight swell of flesh in the dark,
the breath you hold before crying out.
I'm trying to remember that sound but I don't know
what time it is in the place you are.
The small nun appears and disappears
behind the paper screen. She moves slowly now
and I can't hear her as I once did. This garden is how she thinks.
When do you wake and sleep, what eat and drink?

Solitude is presence. It is the absence
I live in now. How long have we lived apart?
A week, a month, a year?   It all feels the same.
Time doesn't move but for the day and the night
moving like a curtain behind the maples. I imagine your hand
on a yellow curtain by a window in the room
where you sleep. The mallard has slipped into shadow
where eelgrass meets sand below the arbutus.
How spend the interval from dawn to dusk?

I don't know. There are nights I go for long walks
in the narrow, twisting streets and stare
at the bare lights in windows as they flare,
then I come back to my room in the dark
and I sit in the dark for long hours.
How far away. Here there is water and leaves
and I think of your hands and feet, a yellow curtain,
a room of light, or is it dark there now?
What do you work at, read, what do you think?

WHAT BREAKS US

It's night and the hours won't answer me.
I stare through the window. Heavy clouds
have risen from the Pacific and now
throw themselves against the glass mountains
in storm and rain. The slow night
drags me toward morning as if I were a body
pulled raw across wet stones. I am trying
to understand what a man is, trying to find
some goodness at the heart of what I am
but words fail me. They are frail stays to rest
a life upon. A man killed fourteen women.
Is it enough to say just that?
He spared the men. Is it enough
to say, *spared, killed.*
Now the world I understood
is gone and nothing is right.
Somewhere I carry in me a killer too.
There's a storm in my hands tonight.
What is it in a man?
What rage, what hate, what hell of thought
can make him murder beauty?
Fourteen women, one and then another.

He spared the men and now
men live with a question.
Here in the night I am trying to find
a clearing in my mind where I can stand.
I never loved killing,
the deer who stood under the apple tree
I shot at twilight years ago,
the bear who dragged his gutshot blood
into a swamp and who I tracked
and finally killed, my hands shaking
at the wrong I had done to the world.
All my dead are many years ago:
my father murdered, my brother
drowned in blood, and friend after friend

long gone. Each leaving took
a piece of me away. I sometimes think
there's nothing left. It's as if I could
stare through my flesh, see through
these hands that cover my eyes. Death
makes us thin. It breaks our fragile bones.

Today at the university I taught a class of writers.
All young women wanting to learn
what a poem is, how to make one.
They want to make things beautiful.
I watch them as they struggle to find a way
to capture what is at the heart of things,
what they know inside, something
made out of words. To imagine
them dead would break me.
They are everything I love.
They place their stories on the page
and though some of their poems are dark
they always bring a light
to heal what might have broken them
when they were only girls: lost love,
lost lives, lost innocence. They are witness
to what they know and they tell us
that we might hear and be made whole at last.

Saying that will get me through the dark.
The storm in me will pass.
The clouds will fall at last and the wind die.
I am a man who's held death in his hands
and I will hold it forever.
The bullet will enter my father's heart
and he will die over and over...
my brother too.
But the young women will come again,
proud and tough and clean as quickened light,
delicate as beauty. I will give them what I can.
Only they can drive away what breaks us in our bones.
It's what I pray for here in the night alone.

THE DAY

Twenty years and today in the garden I knew
the butterfly's flight is as much device as artifice,
the way the erratic serves the creature best, no bird
able to catch such wandering. What to say?
You are far away in retreat at the monastery
and I am imagining you again. The day is quiet
but for the crows who nag the kittens at their play.

The owl has returned. How I love the small bodies
she drops upon the third stone below the fir tree,
the one that slows you. You must look down
to find it and, in that moment, see the maidenhair,
the way it falls beside the Emperor bamboo.

I stopped among the ferns and feverfew
and you came back to me like a blow
and I was of two minds, owl and feverfew—
both fierce, both sure, both wanting.

Tomorrow I will be in Japan, a world away.
You will still be in retreat.
I feel a soft bewilderment. It makes me stumble,
unsure of where my feet go or my hands.
The butterfly hangs now from one of the last lilies.
The cats sleep in the shade. The owl sleeps in the fir
and the crows mutter on and on. Strange
how beauty enters me. It rains
tomorrow, cloudy, cold. The butterfly gives up
his wandering. Tomorrow in Kyoto
I will sit below a pine and watch a monk
bend with great patience as he kneels in moss
to pick up one by one the fallen needles.

THE DANCE
   (For Sophie)

It is as if our hands keep trying to hold
what we cannot have, as if some other child was there
breathing light into the leaves of the madrona, the brittle ones
who die upon themselves, their fruit forgotten
in the fall. Words stumble toward us
like the children we have lost. My friend surrounds the day,
one safety clean as the knife of night he cut himself with
years ago when he carved his flesh into his own hands
for want of love, thinking of all the blood there was,
and taking it, and his child leans into him
with all she is, the girl having forgotten the child
she was, so that looking at her you can hear her dream.
What thou lovest well remains, and I, in the center
of whatever world there is watch him take his child
into the velvet sea and dance. Broken stone
is how she touches his arms. That way, startled
by the man she will describe when she is old
and holds him like the sea holds stone, her words
the many arms of herself, remembering everything—
the blood, the stone, the sea, and her body's touch
bright as what remains, as my child's body remembers
the many tongues who speak to me, as she speaks to him,
practising what must be done, this step, then that,
a foot moved and a hand, as the old dancers used to do
when they were in their crazed beds, their bodies
the leaves of the madrona in the fall, something
in the music of their skin remembering the dance.

FALSE DAWN
(For Stephen & Susan)

We turn to words because there's not much more
to turn to. *I love you* becomes what I used to call
the dark. I prayed this morning. It wasn't much,
just me and the god I understand. The earliest birds
wake me now and I keep getting up into what
others call false dawn. I know it sweeter.
That's the hard part, knowing darkness is there
and singing anyway. Becoming more
becomes less. It's like an origami dove
chased by a flying child, a kind of solitude
so perfect you keep searching even as you know
there is no cure. I think misery is mostly
what we know. Yet there are days I overflow with love.
My friends are so fragile I'm afraid
to take their hands for fear I'll break them.
This morning I set out the early sprinkler
and out of the darkness robins came
and varied thrushes I thought our cats had killed.
The water from our highest mountains turned
and turned above our earth
and all the birds went under that falling
with everything they had.
Maybe that's the measure.
Maybe in the morning light we pray
and rain falls and we lift to its falling
as if we still had feathers, as if with words
we could scrape the sky clean of every kind of pain.

PRAISE

I come back to praise, the hummingbird in the rain,
that single knot of colour among the dying
blooms of the geranium, another kind of day.
It reminds me of what I saw this morning,
a woman leaning out a window, naked, her breasts
no longer young, slack with the loss that comes
from a child's suckling. She was staring down
into the flowers she had planted in the window box,
blue lobelia swaying like a kind of sky,
geraniums, the weight of their blooms, like fists
of men who fought with their hands bare,
knuckles rich with blood. She
did not know I was watching, or if she knew,
didn't care. What she wanted was another
kind of praise, the kind where, if she arranged it,
could make the flowers in her mind alive,
like the ones she saw when she was just a girl
and the whole world heat and waiting.
I thought in the thin shade how, if we were lovers,
her breasts might rest upon my palms
or in my mouth, those nipples on my tongue
and feeding there as she leaned and stared
past me at the light in the window and the flowers.
All this, and the hummingbird, the flare
of his feathers vibrating there, his body
bringing back to me her flesh, his tongue
deep in the blossom, that fierce honey
I want to praise, crying out as I do
in the thing I have called memory and trying
to remember, the rain all around me.

SMALL BIRDS AS RARE AS WISDOM

Small birds as rare as wisdom when they die.
But what we want is something in our arms,
that falling into flesh, the holding after love
when the body gives us a small grace,
the rag in the heart we take and wring.
It is the gypsy in the square in Barcelona,
the one who danced with a wine glass on his head.
He was so perfectly alone. He was as rare
as any bird, as rare as the old man
who sat apart, watching,
making the day with his hands,
a cigarette, a glass of thick red wine,
his eyes as much the dance as the gypsy,
so young you'd think the square belonged
to what he didn't know was grief,
not yet. The old man's eyes. So much the fledglings
who fly in heavy weather, the need
to have such pain rain down on us and then
to lie alone licking anyone's wounds,
even in the night, our own.

THE SOUND

The voice you hear is the sound
inside the emptiness of a great bell.
It is just before the monk comes
from the cloisters to stand below
the curved bronze in the silence
far above him waiting.

GOD WALKS BURNING THROUGH ME

When I sleep the birds come to the garden
with their gifts of seeds. Out of ice

last year's leaves of grass lift into night.
All my songs have been one song.

The palm of my hand and the sole of my foot
remember everything I have forgotten.

The old lantern by the pond has always been there.
Now is the time to light it.

THE SEALING

This is for your eyes alone. I have folded
the paper precisely, one third and then another,
and placed the parchment in its envelope. Here
I place my seal. I heat the honeyed wax and watch it
drip by drip until it forms a liquid pool on the seal
and then I take my hand and make it into a fist
and, standing, press my whole body down
until my house is made here, my seal, my insignia,
my mark, my making. These are my words.
You are the one I have made
them for, in the quiet of my room,
in the dead of night, one word and then another,
and now no one can break it but you.

AFTERWORD

I want to thank The Canada Council and The BC Arts Council for giving me the time to write these poems. I especially want to thank my companion, Lorna Crozier. She has saved me yet again from verbosity and excess or, at least, I hope so. Special thanks to Harold Rhenisch whose poem, "The Night of My Conception," inspired the poem with the same title in this collection. And finally thanks to my mother, Dixie Lane, who read poetry to me in her womb and for the years after I arrived at one minute past midnight sixty-one years ago in 1939. She was fierce and proud and beautiful. Her own childhood was one of abuse, something I only discovered a few years ago. It explained much to me. Her protection, care, and love were only a few of the things she gave her family. She gave birth to three poets, Richard, John, and myself, three brothers born before the Second World War. Her last words to me were, "At every turn there's always something lovely." She, like my father, was much alone. I offer this quotation in her memory:

> *"...By the Nine Gods he swore*
> *That the great house of Tarquin*
> *Should suffer wrong no more..."*

—Thomas Babington Macaulay, "Horatius"

ACKNOWLEDGEMENTS:

CBC Radio
Southern Review (USA)
Prairie Fire
Grain
Descant
The Malahat Review
Meanjin (Japan)
Praise – a chapbook from Reference West